MAKE IT!

Smartphone Movies

Ray Reyes

Rourke
Educational Media

rourkeeducationalmedia.com

SUPPLIES TO COMPLETE ALL PROJECTS:

- printer or copy machine to print additional copies of the screenplay to share with people who will be in your movie
- smartphone and its camera app
- smartphone editing app, like iMovie for iPhones, or Adobe Premiere Clip for Android devices
- backpacks, duffel bags, old suitcases
- blankets and old curtains
- bottled water (optional)
- computer, laptop, or tablet to write your screenplay (optional)
- corkboard and thumbtacks (optional)
- desktop video editing software (optional)
- dry erase board (optional)
- hats, masks, scarves you find in your house
- index cards
- insect repellent (optional)
- JOBY GorillaPod (optional)
- large work area if you are brainstorming and writing the screenplay with other people (optional)

- notebooks or pads of paper
- old Halloween costumes
- old toys, such as plastic swords
- pens or pencils
- portable smartphone charger (optional)
- Scotch tape (optional)
- selfie stick (optional)
- smartphone tripod and mount (optional)
- storyboard template found free online (optional)
- sunscreen (optional)

Table of Contents

Smartphone Movies

A search for buried treasure, superheroes saving the day or a science fiction epic—the sky is the limit. Use a smartphone, editing apps, and everyday items around the house to make fun, entertaining movies with family and friends!

Write a screenplay or draw a **storyboard** for homemade movies you can film on any smartphone. Find the perfect location to match the plot of your movie. Upload your movie to YouTube or other social media sites to share with family and friends.

Write the Screenplay

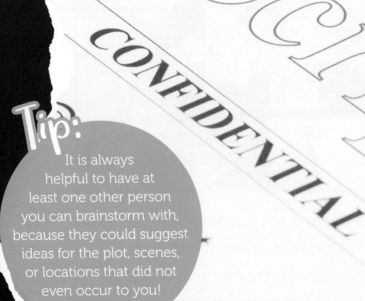

Tip:
It is always helpful to have at least one other person you can brainstorm with, because they could suggest ideas for the plot, scenes, or locations that did not even occur to you!

START WRITING YOUR MOVIE!
Here's How:

1. Decide on the story you want to tell. Will it be a search for buried pirate treasure? Astronauts that land on an alien planet? Superheroes saving the city from an evil mastermind?

2. Create characters for your movie. Who are the heroes? Who are the villains?

3. Write descriptions of the characters and draw pictures of them so you know their personalities and how they look.

Tip:
The plot does not have to be complicated. Keep it simple. Some of the best movie plots are built around the main characters on a quest to save people or retrieve an object.

When writing the setting, remember to describe the exact setting and time of day. That way, when you are filming the movie, you are keeping the plot and chronology of the movie in order.

4. Name your characters. Do not use names from other movies, books, or television shows. Come up with unique names.

5. Write the setting. Be specific. Is it day or night? Sunny or stormy? Details count.

6. Write lines for the characters. Make sure the lines fit each character's personality. For example, you can have lines for the main character—a heroic type—that describes the plot, then write funny lines for a supporting character whose quirk is to always crack jokes when reacting to what the main character said.

7. Print enough copies of the screenplay for everyone involved, even people who won't be filmed. That way everyone knows the story and the order of the scenes.

8. Assemble your cast. Contact the people you want to portray the characters.

9. Once the cast is assembled, gather everyone together at one place to do a table read. That's Hollywood talk for the actors sitting around a table to read and practice their lines. It gives the actors an opportunity to ask questions about the plot and the characters.

Why Is Writing a Screenplay Important?

The screenplay is a guide for what the movie is about, containing descriptions of scenes and settings. Screenplays also have lines for the actors in the movies, key sentences that move the plot along or explain what's happening in the movie.

Storyboard the Movie

CREATE A STORYBOARD!

Here's How:

1. Hollywood filmmakers typically draw pictures of scenes from the screenplay to help them **visualize** how each shot will look on camera. This process is called "storyboarding" a movie.

2. Make your own storyboards by drawing on the back, blank side of index cards to help you visualize a specific scene or an action sequence.

Tip:

You don't have to be an artist to storyboard your movie. You can simply draw stick figures of the characters to help you see how they will stand or move in each scene.

3. Sketch out each scene from your screenplay on one index card at a time, keeping in mind that how you draw the scenes will be how you film and frame the scenes using the smartphone camera.

4. Once you have each scene drawn, tack them, in order, to the corkboard. If you're using a big dry erase board, tape them in order on the board.

Tip:
If you don't have a big enough corkboard or dry erase board, simply place your storyboards on the floor in order or tape them to a wall.

5. Look at your completed storyboards. It's a visual representation of your screenplay! The storyboards give you an idea of how your movie will look before you even start filming.

6. If a scene looks out of place or out of order, you can move individual index cards around to achieve a better sense of how the story flows. Hollywood filmmakers do this all the time.

Tip: If you do move some storyboards around, remember to add this as a note in your screenplay. You may come up with a cool scene during the storyboarding process, so add the note or the scene in the screenplay so you don't forget!

7. Now that you have your completed storyboards, take them down from the boards or the wall and stack them in chronological order.

8. Take the storyboards and screenplay with you for the next step: finding locations for your movie.

Why Is Storyboarding Important?

Drawing each scene of the movie and placing them on a large surface helps you visualize the written words of your screenplay. It also helps your cast to see where they will stand and move in each shot and how each scene will flow into the next.

Scout Locations

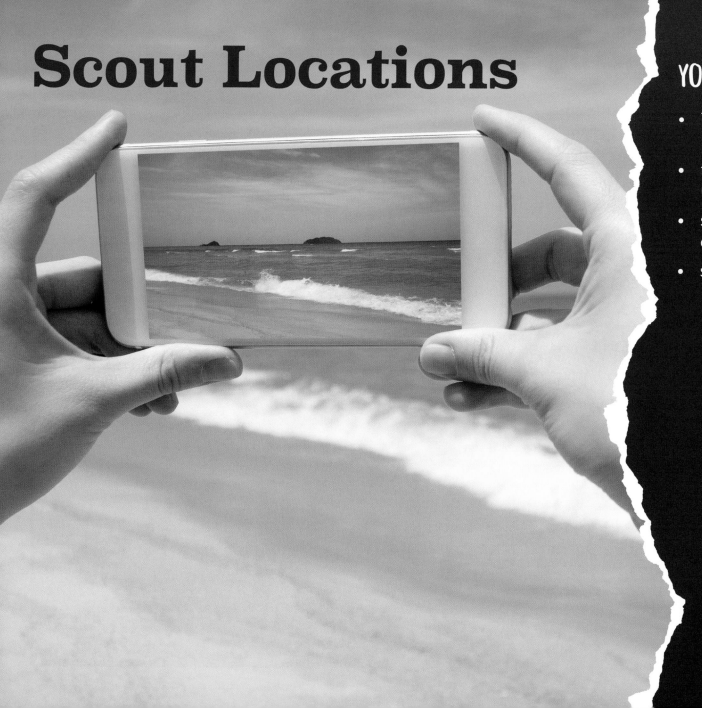

FIND THE PERFECT LOCATION FOR YOUR MOVIE!

Here's How:

1. Go with family members or friends to an outdoor area to see if it could work as a backdrop or location for your movie. This is called location scouting.

2. Depending on how many scenes you have in your screenplay, you might need more than one location.

3. Be creative! A local park with a playground, a forest in a state park, the beach, sidewalks and alleys in your downtown area or even a nearby creek could be the perfect setting for your movie.

Tip: Keep the locations close together. You will have many people with you, including your cast members and relatives. You want to have fun and not stress about running around to multiple locations far away from each other!

4. Take a smartphone photo of every interesting setting you see. When you start filming your movie, you can refer to these photos so you know the exact location for each scene.

5. You can even print out the photos and add them to your screenplay notes or storyboards. This may help you visualize your movie better.

Tip:

Don't forget the insect repellent, sunscreen, and bottled water! You will be outdoors during your location scouting, and you may need these items to be comfortable.

6. Have indoor locations as a backup plan in case the weather does not cooperate on filming day. A local community center is a perfect location, provided you ask permission first. Your teachers may even allow you to use the classroom or the school auditorium. Your house or a friend's house could work as well.

Why Is Location Scouting Important?

Visiting locations before you film your movie helps you narrow down the best settings to tell your story. Having the locations selected beforehand also makes shooting day easier.

Create and Find Props

USE EVERYDAY ITEMS AROUND YOUR HOUSE FOR MOVIE PROPS!

Here's How:

1. The **genre** of your movie influences what type of everyday objects you can use as props.

2. For example, if you're filming a movie about superheroes, old blankets and curtains can make great capes.

3. If your screenplay is about the search for buried treasure, a jar of pennies in an old suitcase can represent the treasure.

Tip:
If you can't find certain items around the house, ask permission to go to a thrift store or a yard sale. You can find great items there without spending a lot of money.

4. If your movie is science fiction, you may have some old toys around your house that you can use.

5. If you're filming an adventure movie, cargo shorts or pants, along with a vest with plenty of pockets are quick props you can use to have the look of an explorer. An old camera would also make an excellent prop for such characters.

6. Masks, gloves, and scarves can also round out the look of your characters.

Tip:
Be creative! Everyday objects make great movie props if you use your imagination!

Why Are Props So Important?

Costumes and props, even those made from everyday items, help make your movie feel more believable. The right props, paired with the settings you have scouted, enhance the story you're telling.

Film Your Movie

YOU WILL NEED:

- JOBY Gorillapod (optional)

- portable smartphone charger (optional)

- selfie stick (optional)

- smartphone

- smartphone tripod and mount (optional)

RECORD SCENES WITH A SMARTPHONE!

Here's How:

1. You've assembled your cast. You've scouted your locations. You have your costumes and props. Now it's time to start filming your movie!

2. Using the screenplay and storyboards, record each scene of the movie using the smartphone's standard video app.

3. Record multiple takes of each scene. You can edit the best takes together later.

4. If you do not have someone who can hold the smartphone, use a tripod and a tripod mount. A tripod keeps the recording image steady and stationary, so the camera doesn't shake and blur the images.

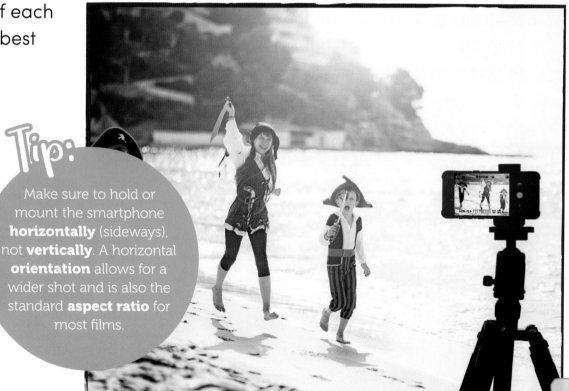

Tip:

Make sure to hold or mount the smartphone **horizontally** (sideways), not **vertically**. A horizontal **orientation** allows for a wider shot and is also the standard **aspect ratio** for most films.

5. If you have a selfie stick, mount the smartphone on it and let one character hold it. The shot from a higher angle might make for an interesting image.

6. Shoot a lot of footage. Shoot more than you need. It is always a good idea to have plenty of recorded footage, so you can edit the strongest scenes together after you film the movie.

7. Allow for **improvisation**. Sometimes you don't have to follow the script! One of your actors may say a line that's not in the screenplay and it's so good or so funny that you decide to leave it in the movie.

Tip:
Smartphone video apps drain the battery quickly. If you have a portable smartphone charger, bring it on location so you can record for much longer.

Edit Your Movie

EDIT YOUR RAW FOOTAGE!

Here's How:

1. Open the video editing app on the smartphone. The first thing you want to do is create a new project then add all the clips you recorded into the project.

2. Smartphone video editing applications offer helpful tips. Tap the "help" or "question mark" icon. The app's on-screen prompts will guide you with the next steps.

3. The "help" icon also highlights the various tools you can use to make a polished movie. These include trimming scenes, adding transitions to scenes, or even adding colored filters to give your movie a unique look.

Tip: Editing a movie is a technical process, even on a smartphone. Take your time. Be patient. Become familiar with all the features in the video editing app. If you need more help, do an Internet search for video editing tips.

4. After you edit the best takes into a movie that matches your screenplay and storyboards, consider adding music or sound effects to your scenes.

5. iMovie for iTunes and other editing apps have music you can use. Add the music by tapping the section of clips where you want it to start (usually it's the "playhead," the white vertical line that appears over your clips) then tapping the "add media" button.

6. In the "add media" menu, you can preview, then select "theme music and sound effects."

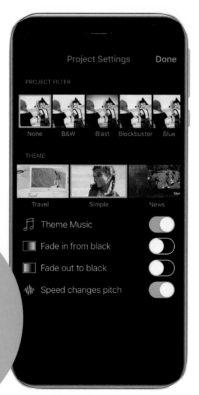

Tip: If you have more than an hour of recorded footage, it may be easier to transfer the clips from the smartphone to a desktop computer's video editing software.

Show Off Your Movie to the World

FINISH YOUR MOVIE AND HAVE A PREMIERE PARTY!

Here's How:

1. Save your movie and export it as a completed project.

2. Ask your parents to help you create an account for a social media site such as YouTube, Vimeo, or a family member's Facebook account.

3. Email the link to your movie to family and friends.

Tip: You can have a premiere party at your house. Simply load your movie on a laptop, or copy the movie to a USB thumb drive and plug it into a smart TV. Let everyone gather around to watch your first movie. Don't forget the popcorn!

Glossary

aspect ratio (AS-pekt REY-sho): the ratio of the width of an image to its height, usually a standard ratio such as 16 to 9 or 4 to 3

genre (ZHAHN-ruh): a class or category of artistic endeavor having a particular form, content or technique

horizontally (hawr-uh-ZON-tel-ee): at right angles to the vertical; parallel to level ground

improvisation (im-prov-uh-ZEY-shuhn): the act of composing, uttering, executing or arranging anything without previous preparation

orientation (awr-ee-uhn-TEY-shuhn): the direction or position of a particular object

storyboard (STOHR-ee-baord): a panel or panels on which a sequence of sketches depict the significant changes of action and scene in a film

vertically (VUR-ti-kuhl-ee): standing upright

visualize (VIZH-oo-uh-layz): to form a mental image of

Index

Show What You Know

1. Why should you write a screenplay?

2. Why is it important to use storyboards?

3. Why should you scout locations before you film a movie?

4. Why should you use props?

5. Explain how improvisation can strengthen a scene.

Further Reading

Blofield, Robert, *How to Make a Movie in 10 Easy Lessons*, Walter Foster Jr, 2016.

Willoughby, Nick, *Digital Filmmaking for Kids*, John Wiley & Sons Inc, 2015.

www.minimoviemakers.com

About the Author

Ray Reyes is a freelance photographer, former newspaper reporter, and backyard astronomer. He frequently goes out in the middle of the night to photograph stars and the Milky Way. In his free time, he enjoys reading, spending time with family and friends, traveling, and binge-watching television shows.

Meet The Author!
www.meetREMauthors.com

PHOTO CREDITS: Cover: © creativelytara; Page 4: © Pixsooz, mediaphotos, Ittollmater, Imgorthand; Page 5: © Imgorthand, Blackzheep; Page 6: © Pixsooz; Page 7: © milanvirijevic, Marilyn Nieves; Page 8:© Pixsooz; Page 9: © vgajic; Page 10: © mediaphotos; Page 11: © Erdak; Page 12: © asiseeit; Page 13: © hatman12, akarakingdoms; Page 14: © Valeri Kovtoen, akarakingdoms; Page 15:© Ittollmatar; Page 16: © Imgorthand; Page 17: © Ittollmatar, Dmitri Maruta; Page 18: vgajic; Page 19–21: © Imgorthand; Page 22: © Imgorthand, Blackzheep; Page 23: © Imgorthand, Daniel Chetroni; Page 24: © Imgorthand, Blackzheep; Page 25: © Imgorthand, Bongkarn Thanyakij; Page 26–27: © Ivcandy, Imgorthand; Page 28: © FatCamera, Imgorthand; Page 29: © FatCamera

Edited by: Keli Sipperley
Cover and Interior design by: Tara Raymo • CreativelyTara • www.creativelytara.com

Library of Congress PCN Data

Smartphone Movies / Ray Reyes
(Make It!)
ISBN 978-1-64156-442-7 (hard cover)
ISBN 978-1-64156-568-4 (soft cover)
ISBN 978-1-64156-687-2 (e-Book)
Library of Congress Control Number: 2018930470

Rourke Educational Media
Printed in the United States of America,
North Mankato, Minnesota